Wisteria

Other Titles by Kwame Dawes

Wisteria

Twilight Poems from the Swamp Country

Kwame Dawes

RED HEN PRESS LOS ANGELES

WISTERIA

Cover art: From *A True Likeness: The Black South of Richard Samuel Roberts*
(Columbia, SC Bruccoli Clark Layman, 1986)

Book design by Michael Vukadinovich
Cover Design by Mark E. Cull

ISBN: 1-59709-059-X
Library of Congress Catalog Card Number: 2005933596

The City of Los Angeles Cultural Affairs Department, California Arts
Council, Los Angeles County Arts Commission and National
Endowment for the Arts partially support Red Hen Press.

First Edition

for
Lorna, Sena, Kekeli, and Akua

for
Gwyneth, Kojo, Aba, Adjoa and Kojovi
for
Mama the Great

And remembering
Neville

Acknowledgements

I thank Lana Odom, my guide to finding home in Sumter, South Carolina. She opened the way for me to meet the elders of Manning Avenue and the Southside. They told me their stories in the South Sumter Resource Center, sending me away every day with a fever to make poems, to tell their stories and to keep their voices alive. Thanks to these men and women—in their seventies and eighties who, ten years ago, taught me something about being southern and black: Mrs. Odom, Mrs. Jones, Mrs. Richardson, Mrs. Sanders, Mrs. Tarlton, Mr. Ross, and Reverend Thrower. These poems are not transcriptions of their voices, but a rendering that comes through our shared language of the Middle Passage and the many journeys we have all taken.

Thanks also to those who helped me to shape this manuscript—Holly Schullo, Ellen Arl and Charlene Spearen. Give thanks to Colin Channer and Justine Henzel—always reminding me of what we can do. Thanks especially to Kevin Simmonds for his beautiful musical rendering of so many of these poems and for helping me to see these poems in fresh ways. Thanks to the Columbia Museum of Art for hosting the first performance of *Wisteria: Twilight Songs from the Swamp Country.* Thanks to Chris Abani for making the big link. Special thanks to the kind and brilliant crew at the inimitable Red Hen Press. And Thanks to the Department of English at the University of South Carolina for allowing me the space and time to write—*One love.*

Grateful acknowledgement to the following publications in which some of these poems have appeared in some form: *Callaloo, Atlanta Journal and Constitution, Poetry London, Obsidian III, Point, Doubletake Magazine,* and *The Lettered Olive.* Several of these poems appeared in *Midland* (Ohio University Press, 2001) and in *New and Selected Poems* (Peepal Tree, 2003). *Wisteria* has been set to music by Kevin Simmonds and performed live in several venues.

Kwame Dawes
Columbia, SC 2005

Contents

Three / Domestics

Four / Vengeance

Five / Obituaries

Wisteria

Naked

For Billy Baldwin

It dawned on me, flaming new sun—
there is a knife blade of wisdom in this sighting,
it cuts too deep—I am still caught
in the slippery rain slick road, the caution sign
illuminated by my wandering lights:
my eyes are still too mute for night driving,
but on this precarious road it dawned:
this is the problem of race in this country,
layering, like clothes in winter,
folks wear layers and layers to block it out
to keep it all in, and only the heat
cooling into insane crispy ferocity can make 'em
strip to the pale vulnerable bare
of the flesh, hands covering genitals, chests
twitching with the fear of eyes—
vulnerable like this, there is nothing to hold
like an axe over our heads, and all
there is is the flow of tears. This is the taste
of fear. Why people wear clothes.
We are so used to the heat, to dancing
naked in the sunlight, to be seen
prodded, pushed, exposed, studied, we forget
we have not seen them stale and alone
in the blazing sun. So strip them, I say,
all suits, shoes, hats, shirts, briefs
gathered, burnt, let them stand there and watch
us watch them, there. We will learn
something of the mortal vanity of our humanity,
something of the bareness of their power,
and then we will watch them eat grass.
It is the way of the world.

One

Wisteria

Wisteria

Circumspect woman,
you carry your memories
tied up in a lip-stick-stained
kerchief in a worn straw basket.
When you undo the knot,
the scent of wisteria,
thick with the nausea of nostalgia
fills the closed-in room.

You lean into the microphone,
smile at the turning tape,
while fingering the fading petals.
You intone your history,
breathing in the muggy
scent of wayward love.
Your anger is always
a whisper, enigmatic,
almost unspoken,
just a steady heat.

I don't like 'em
never did, never could . . .

Recreation

At seven o'clock in high summer,
there was still light bleeding
in the nigger sky.
The twilight silence swelled;
we felt the tickle of North wind
coming off the Santee river.

Birds swooped down into the yard,
dancing around the snare
left out by my father
who was snoring his life away
behind the hog pens
upwind, where the air was fresh.
The birds reading the clues,
turned in mute animation,
caught the wind and flew.

To pass the time
we made love in the bush.
I stared at the faded line
of a coming moon.

I have not heard such silence
as that secret meeting,
everything whispered,
then grunts and stifled gasps;
never heard such silence
since I took off from those cotton groves
that year they exploded Pearl Harbor
and our boys went to spill their blood
among the bamboo and coconuts.

Nowadays, the mutter of radios,
staccato talk of television
and the drone of engines
on the interstates
frighten away the ghosts.

I no longer hear
in the swollen dumb season
the thud of horse hooves
coming, stallions snorting
something ghastly like
Revelations,
beating to my heart's pulse
thumping after the flicker
of excitement of his hand
on me, the feel of his trembling.

I still recall those idle dusks
when we waited for night to come
upon us quickly, and then slept.

Tornado Child

For Rosalie Richardson

I am a tornado child.
I come like a swirl of black
and darken up your day;
I whip it all into my womb,
lift you and your things,
carry you to where you've never been
and maybe, if I feel good,
I might bring you back,
all warm and scared,
heart humming wild like a bird
after early sudden flight.

I am a tornado child.
I tremble at the elements.
When thunder rolls
my mother-womb trembles,
remembering the tweak of contractions
that tightened to a wail
when my mother pushed me out
into the black of a tornado night.

I am a tornado child,
you can tell us from far,
by the crazy of our hair;
couldn't tame it if we tried.
Even now I tie a bandanna
to silence the din of anarchy
in these coir-thick plaits.

I am a tornado child
born in the whirl of clouds;
the centre crumbled,
then I came. My lovers
know the blast
of my chaotic giving;
they tremble at the whip
of my supple thighs;
tornado child, you cross me
at your peril, I cling to light
when the warm of anger
lashes me into a spin,
the pine trees bend to me
swept in my gyrations.

I am a tornado child.
When the spirit takes my head,
I hurtle into the vacuum
of white sheets billowing
and paint a swirl of colour,
streaked with my many songs.

Courting

At fifteen and bold-eyed,
I was a married woman.
My man came along
like any casual day comes along,
did a simple transaction;
too trustworthy to call it love.
And Mama said,
"It's time,
you still got your looks,
you got a body, too,
you got no future
but cooking for white folks;
you meet a man
wants to make a family
let him have you
the right way
of course"

At fifteen, never dreamed
romance would come,
and I was right.
Never dreamed of dates,
movies, fancy restaurants,
and I was right.
Didn't miss much
cause you only miss
what you dreamed too much.

At sixteen, didn't know
the rhythm of my body;
nobody told me what it was
that bad feeling that would take me
early before light
like grease from fat-back
sitting heavy on your chest;
but I could tell it was something
not to talk too much about;
like the way my husband
took me all those nights,
talking soft, touching soft,
telling me to hush.

So I said it was a headache
when the doctor comes round,
and the poor man so ashamed
that nice bright handsome boy,
he gave me something for the headache,
and whisper the news to my man,
who told me when the doctor was gone.
And how I cried the day,
not for the love of a child in me,
not for the joy of the woman in me,
but for the shame of my foolish self
country girl, real country girl.

Hawk

Old Mama talked with her fingers,
sipped her liquor till time stopped.

Old Mama smiled rueful days,
whispered her secrets always

to the faithful wind, always going
some place, coming back forgetful

every time, of whose lips it had kissed,
whose secrets tasted at midnights.

We have lost Mama to the wind.
She left clothes, shoes, pills

and a bag of funky stories behind,
buried in her underthings, her hair-pins.

Putting her away, smelling her presence
we break into songs, weaving her sentences

together, like the clumpy plaits she made
of our hair in the soft of kerosene light.

At the grave-side, we stare at the swoop
of predator jets, circling the Base,

and Maude walks with Mama's limp,
favouring her right ankle, like Mama did,

muttering 'bout the way it twisted when she ran
from the snort of a white stallion

on that slate gray Carolina dawn
when the cotton fields were blanched,

and the wind was passing by, quiet-quiet,
the diving hawks still screaming.

DEM

Never called a white man *massa*,
never called no white woman *missus*,
just plain old *sir* and m'*am*,
like I would for any soul whose got
age enough to make me feel like a child.

And just how *daddy* is like *sir*,
how when you speak it you think of God
staring down hard at your body minding
its own business and growing all them hairs
and letting things flow inside of you
making you feel things you never should
and your mouth muttering sin all the while.

Just like that, every time I would
stare at the scraggly grass, dry summer bush
on the edge of the cotton rows,
eye-balling a pebble sitting lonely there
in the sun, just waiting for me to find it
leaning soft against my toes,
under the ragged shadow of our home
looming cool and dark, eating up
the shape of a man on a horse
whose eyes I can't see, 'cause I'm staring
at the way the earth grows dark at dusk.

Just like that, every time I spoke
the word *Mister* to bossman Creech,
was like my soul tensing for a crack
of his tongue, like my body saying,
yes *suh, massa, no suh, massa*
I will jus' step over yonder and fetch it, massa;
and I could feel his eyes on my head;
could tell he knew the shame of me,
feeling naked there before him and all.

I don't call them nothing no more;
they is just man, woman, dem,
that's all they is, that's all.

Banking

In the cold season
we bank love like potatoes
cashing in on them
when the wind
whips sorrow
like the bitter
leaf of purging.

Mama pulls from mounds of straw
the firm yellowness of sustenance,
then boiling the skinned flesh
in the pot, she offers us her love.

It is all memory
now, this other
life, when cold
rattled our bones
and love was
the predictability
of daily bread,
the quench of river-water.

We have buried their still bodies
in the swamp earth among
the pine needles and dark loam.
I offer songs at the grave, like love proffered.

Time

Not too old to feel the bile,
that back-breaking anger,
that feeling of death in my heart.

Not too old to turn on their smiles,
transparent thin things,
wanting to raise an open palm; to strike.

Not too old to watch an ancient one of them
lament the encasing of her man,
the jutting-bellied cracker, and smile . . .

Not too old to count their graves
like notches of God's blessing, to say;
"Shit, I outlived you, I outlived you."

Not too old to still my tongue,
to hum a blue gospel, while my soul
sings that old cry of motherlessness.

Not too old to dream of blood,
the taste of iron on my lips,
the swell of power in my breast.

Not too old to hear the nightriders,
to face the starched sheets of this South,
with trembling, with the heart of a child.

Not too old, not too old,
not too old, not too old.

Still Born

Take my baby home,
Take my baby home,
I ain't free, and never will be,
Take my baby home.

I still count them, feeling them like ghost limbs.
They have their place in my collection of years.
Remembering them is a way to remember
to count the pressure pills,
the heart pills, the blood pills,
the tyranny of pills.

I count those who died before they woke,
those I cradled, caressed, cocooned to life,
hoping beyond the weakness of their cries.
They died, too, leaving us with tough questions
for God Almighty. Old Black folk have buried
so many babies in the bush behind the cotton
groves, with the naked form of cotton bales,
standing like sentinel crucifixes
against the stale blue of summer skies.

Oh, Glory,
Oh, Glory.
There is room enough
In Paradise
To have a home.

And mother gathers her body and the tears,
and builds new fires, cooks new meals,
readies her womb to replenish
its rooted self to make more brothers, sisters
like second nature. She carries her moaning
deep in her skin, a way to count the days.

My mother bore nine children—
we chant this as a litany of her strength.
Three did not live to see the second year
of her wash-belly, wash-soul, wash-body,
the thin film of her drying birth waters,
scraped off with a rough cloth
as they laid her out to rest.

Sometimes I feel
Like a motherless child,
A long way from home,
A long way from home.

Gender

The first time I came
my heart faded quickly
and the plans of my father,
sensing the lifting of his load,
drifted away in a chill morning.
They planted my body,
my shriveled manhood,
curled like a worm.

When I came again,
castrated and thick-lashed,
my father counted his losses
and helped me grow the callous
of my hands, building
by his side the edifice
of our modest existence,
he did not see the coming
of my bleeding, man-child that I was.

But the boys could smell
the flaring of my womb,
could sniff their thirst-quencher
as I dragged the plough
through fallow ground. They would stare
at my cupped breasts as I ran,
leaping the low hedges of peanut bushes.
Their laughter, hands feeling at crotches,
tongues moistening the gleaming strands
of fledgling mustaches,
made me turn and run.

In the city, the wind played
whimsy with my bare thighs,
the soft fabric on my skin.
Here, the boys moved slower,
casual eyes recording me woman,
not taboo, homoerotic enigma,
simply woman walking the city streets
and my smile was big as light.

Dreaming

Today on the news, the woman
with a face bloated
from old whiskey and rut-gut,
said in that drawling, hung-over,
dead-pan, sure-as-hell-lying way:

"I didn't do it, I swear to God, I didn't . . . "

Still I know as clear as memory, I know
how she and her husband, the bandy-legged,
swollen-bellied spitter of tobacco juice
on a cement floor, buzzing with green flies,
fed off the waste and blood of some
caught black boy, who thought he could
play wrestling games with their white son,
and how they whipped him for that game real bad.

I know how they slapped him around, spat on him,
pissed on him, till he collapsed
and they let him fall. He did not see them
waddling their sour selves
into the trailer, all rusted,
broken, and leaning still from old storms,
to finish the beer and whiskey,
then falling into fitful sleep
in the soft, smoky sofa.

Imagine them dreaming of another time
when the orgasmic sweet of his final
scream before the breath floated into the swamp
air; how they groaned at the memory.

I went to sleep in the wake of the news,
my eyes closed, but strange lights
danced across my blindness.
I thought I had forgotten the pulse of hate
until the thick flame of acid
burnt my throat and I retched,
tears for the boy, still trembling
still smelling his own stool.

"I didn't do it, I swear to God, I didn't . . . "

Jesus will I die in peace,
or will I wake always to the pain
of another tooth being yanked from my jaw?

Long Memory

And if it is not hate
it must be something
more insidious than hate,
something like the cold
nonchalance with which
small boys slaughter lizards,
must be something
like the casual bloodletting
of livestock at the butchery.

The sheriff does not suspect
hate in the stringing-up
of a nine year old, choking him
beating him—no hate there
in calling him "Little nigger shit!"
No hate in that at all,
just drunken mischief,
for this is the sport of couples
there in Mount Zion
in the dry cold January low country.

How can I explain to you
that I have searched their eyes
and it is still there, the light,
that tells me all this is at the edge
of their precarious lives? How can I
tell you that I still weep
at the news of such cruelty?

My father brought home the news
of a lynched family friend in such
cold whispers that we all mourned
in deepest silence through the night
that closed, inscrutable mantle
around us. My father stared into
the fading embers of our home fires,
silent as a stone in water.

Skin

This skin is leather black with time,
this skin is tough like old rooster flesh,
this skin won't give like poulet,
you bite this skin you likely to eat crow,
this skin has wailed its own symphony
of blue black sorrow, tough like this,
this skin tasted the salt crystals,
licked them up and recorded the pain,
this skin's been turned inside out, left to dry,
this skin's swallowed the blast of sun,
collected the bite of January air
and still there, still there,
this skin has smelt the acrid smoke
of burning flesh, hanging there against
a new day, sniffed it, felt its layering
of old skin, soot carrying centuries
of suffering, this skin is washed with flow
of menstrual blood, love juice, old semen,
bitter spit, loose shit, every ugliness
dumped into the earth been through this skin,
this is no tenderloin, prime cut skin,
you bite me, you likely to eat crow,
this skin is a walking museum,
when you see me coming read me
when you see me coming read me.

One day I will come to the river.
Oh, love will touch this skin,
and I will rise, ebony glow and tender
crossing that river to the other side.

Script

You can't pick enough cotton
to crawl your way out the hole
your well-deep belly
and that of your litter
done dig for you.

Pricking each payment
in the black-bound ledger,
God, red-eyed and with a cavernous mouth,
breasts that sag and a gut like at sixty
she could be pregnant again
with another messiah,
tells you about the grace
she's been meting out to you
to keep you through the winter.

This earth is your prison.
Your cotton floats into a hole.
The train howls "Chicago!"
How to escape this heaven
of mercy, grace and trust.

When your Daddy died,
they called in the eldest son,
all twelve years old of him,
told him what he owed,
set him to toil
so he could taste the grace
of their monthly ciphering.

You can't pick enough cotton
to crawl your way out the hole,
your long-bellied, nigger self
done dug all these centuries,
and God saying, "My grace is sufficient,"
while the train howls, "Chicago!"

Black Funk

The rigid of my jaw bone
is power forged in the oven
of every blow I have felt.
My water walk is something like
compensation for a limp.
Don't begrudge me my sashay
walk, it's all I got sometimes.

'Cause I know the way you stare,
pale blue eyes like a machete edge
catching the colour of new sky,
the way you barely whisper
your orders, spit out the food,
complain about my shuffling gait,
snorting out my funky smell,
find fault in each task I do,
never right, never good enough,
curse my children like dogs,
cause I know you just hurting
drooling your bitterness
when my back is turned,
when the shape of my black ass
swings that way you hate,
sashaying through this room of daggers.

I know you're wondering what I've got
down there, in my belly, in my thighs,
make him leave your side,
crawl out of his pale sick skin
and howl like a beast at night,
whimper like a motherless babe
suckling on me, suckling on me.

You can't hide the shame you feel
to know I sometimes turn him back.
I know you know it, from the way,
he comes on you hard and hurried,
searching for a hole to weep his soul in—
yes, I turn him back when I want,
and he still comes back for more.
I've got my pride sometimes.

I know the way you try to read me
try to be me, can't be me,
never be me, never feel the black
of me, never know the blues in me,
'cause you never want to see you
in me even though we bleed together,
finding each other's tidal rhythms,
and bloat together like sisters,
hoarding the waters of the moon together.

So I sashay through your life,
averting the blades with my leather skin.
I abuse you, and when he bawls,
that is my pride at work,
all I've got sometimes.
I'll cook your meals
until he keels over,
and you just have to take it
'cause I took it with no fuss
when he forced his nothing self on me,
while my babies sucked their thumbs
within the sound of my whimpering;
I paid, baby;
I'm just reaping what y'all done sowed.

Memory

Sometime I could sit down
and remember better
than I think I could remember—
from way back—better than I can do now.
I may say something today,
or see something today
or somebody may say something,
and it goes out.

Two

Traveling Woman

Traveling

SS *Cherokee* going to take me
going to take me far
far from the muggy
soft earth mist
of these cotton-picking lands.

Sailing to New York,
where you learn names
of streets like songs.

Leaving behind the farm
and tired, broken folk.

Charleston Harbour,
like a picture book.

Seems I am going far,
the way my feet feel
like walking on water.

The way my feet feel
like walking on water.
Seems I am going far.

I'm a traveling gal.

Scrapbook

Learning the leaves
in the city parks.
Names that boy would let
roll off his tongue
and me catching the sound
of magic in the names.

I plant the flowers
with love in the belly
of my scrapbook
and press in the botany,
the learning, not mine
not this poor country girl's.

After the smell of onions
on the fingers have faded,
I touch the red of roses,
roll the petals in fingertips
and smell the mist
of another life.

In the morning
my body is tender
with travel, soft
with flight and music.

Swamp Song

The boys stare at the *pandies*
like they staring at red candies

want to touch it, lick it,
caress it, take it, own it;

never look at us that way,
never got sweet words to say

to simple colored girls like us
who don't jitterbug, don't ride no horse;

just work till our fingers are white,
stumbling homeward, weary at night.

We all have dreams, I suppose.
Me, I want me some shoes, nice clothes,

a little learning, some sweet love
and a promise of glory up above.

Let them dream of their *pandies*
pale skinned, store-bought candies,

let them taste the intoxication
of their livid imaginations,

and when they grow weary
straining for that *pandy* mystery

they'll come home to the warm and damp
of this sweet soft Carolina swamp.

Work

Sunhot, no wind, dry, dry,
dropping the fuzzy seeds;

planting somebody else's wealth,
waiting for snow to grow

like new life from the ground.

Cool wind biting, with flies,
fingers stiff with callused pricks,

clean up the leprosy of white
on the stretch of green

as far as the eye can see.

I am driving along I-76 to Florence
the groves of old cotton smile back at me.

At Lynchburg a monstrous beast
crawls through the groves reaping

in its wake, specks of disease remain.

Nothing to clean a cotton grove
like trained fingers, sharp eyes;

takes days, takes the shift of your back
and you still wake up groaning;

still dream of the stretch of white on green.

Train Ride

Hard to picture those sweet boys
nameless black boys in the gut

of a slow moving freight train
crawling towards a new place.

Hard to see them take turns
on the pinkness of those white girls.

Still, I see the faces of those two
smiling on the bright newsprint,

making strong men wince
at the thought of this travesty,

their indulgent day-dreams
of rocking to some decadent beat

of the train, nine ejaculations,
nine fallen selves, howling, howling.

Don't have a mind for names,
but I learnt the names of the two:

Ruby Bean and Victoria Price,
like icons of a time past,

heard them carry like songs
in that hall there on 155th Street

and Rockland Palace, where we gathered
to pray for them Scottsboro boys,

to pray for their souls, forgiveness for
their dumb sin of watching those girls

with fiddling and more on their minds,
with the taste of taboo salivating their mouths.

Victoria Price and Ruby Dean.
I strengthen the pure resolve of my ways,

the intact hymen of my twenty-year old womb,
not loose and wayward like those crazy two.

We cherish the dignity of our righteousness
gleaming white beside the white girls' sin.

No tears for the children, tears are hard
to come by when you've see boys gathered

and whipped and worse for looking too hard,
for thinking of touching, for even smelling

and turning away from the breeze left behind
by white young girls like those two.

All you feel to say is old people's wisdom:
"You make your bed, you lay in it. You know better."

Can't believe those Scottsboro boys
had no idea what history they was messing with

rocking on that old freight train,
cutting through the heart of America.

God Don't Like Ugly

They say God don't like ugly,
and those who make ugly pretty,
they are the angels of God.
Those who can take a shack,

a low down hole with a roof,
and make you want to cry
for the smell of Mama's cooking
the love of days following days

like a sweet-loved baby girl
not fretting about nothing at all,
they are the angels of God.
Those who make ugly pretty.

So I ride through the low country,
day in day out, to the coast, holding
back the waves of sleep creeping up
my legs, like how death comes,

just to learn to make something
prettier than what it was.
Around here, in Sumter County,
we've got two kind of angels:

them that make the dead smile
with powders, creams, lotions,
resting in peace there, prettier than
they ever was when walking this earth;

and them that take complaining hair,
dry back of the hand, facial skin,
and make that pretty as morning,
pretty as a poem there in the salon.

They are the angels of God,
for God don't like ugly at all.
Here in Sumter County, two things are sure,
folks will die their ugly deaths

and women lapping up the magazines
won't ever feel pretty enough for love.
Me, I am too scared of the cold flesh
that don't give back, don't move,

so I caress the women's jowls,
till all they can do is smile
call me angel of the Lord
'cause God don't like ugly.

Dream

In New York state, the farms spread
with familiar patient grace;
the sky is big, a fabric of colors

changing in the dazzling light,
the worn wood of ancient barns,
the timeless drag of farm critters.

In the distance, I see the trail
of a train, crawling south,
naming the mystery of cities,

keys to my heart. I long
for the simple smells of swamp earth,
the fingers of the soil holding me.

In this reverie, dreaming my body
toward the factory where we make bombs
it is easy to forget the dancing lights

circling the stern street-lamp
there on Moore Street, the flashing
scared eyes of the Klansmen; boys

I know I seen naked, heard bawl,
aflame with something searing,
the sick hate of a boy-child for a mother

wanting so much to be a man among men,
willing to slaughter love for the company
of masculine smells, grunts, laughter.

I turn away from the memory, longing
for the swamp only. The train whistles soft
through the big space. Time is still. I linger.

Three

Domestics

At the Lake

Mama,
down by the lake
under the live oaks

the boy punched me
in my belly, I couldn't breathe

everything turned white
'til the lake reached the sky

and him there laughing
face all red with the sun.

So I slapped him
'cross the nose and he wailed.

And you came and grabbed me
shook me up there before all of them

till all I could do was
close my eyes and pretend I was flying

or walking down to the bottom
of the lake where everything is soft,

everything is warm and gentle
like how it is when I crawl in the space

where your body has just been
on a real cold night.

Mama, I could hardly breathe.
How come you gather him up

in your arms, telling him to hush,
all cooing, hush baby, hush honey;

leaving me there in the soggy leaves
to suck my tongue, Mama, how come?

Love Oil

1

I saw how they trimmed you down,
called you Rosie, like a pet dog,

and you smiled and called the boy
same age as me, Mister, like you calling

love. How you grabbed him up from the grass
when fire ants took at us in the yard,

and you made your face like it was
your own feet aflame with sting;

and you bawled me down for being such a fool
for not knowing no better than to take the boy

out into the yard like that, telling me
to go get my legs all washed off

stead of standing there with my eyes all wet
like a fool or something worse.

Saw how you laid him down
and sung your song oiling your palms

soothing him like a baby
his eyes drinking you in.

2
You complain of the arthritis in your legs
when the rain gathers over the swamp,

and I drive through the fog to find you
and fill my hands with sharp Bengay.

And I love those legs, mother, love
those veins, green on your tender yellow skin,

with songs you never sang for me, Mama,
with tender I ever felt for you.

Stations

It's not like y'all domestics was like that,
bowing and scraping, quiet, forgiving;

not Aunt Jasmine who would cuss them,
call them stinking, nasty crackers

while you and her be playing your cards
on Saturday night, sipping your beer,

trying to get back all the dignity you give up
all week-long. But you always would nod,

but never say a evil thing 'bout them;
and when Aunt J. was gone, you would tell the wind

that if she would love her own like they
love their owns, maybe she would be doing better

than drinking all that liquor,
and messing with every man what come her way;

that's how you would say it
out to the wind, quiet-quiet.

Or the time when my titties was fulling out
and the boys start to looking, and he ask me

to touch them, that time when I said no
and I started to tell y'all how sick he was,

and Aunt Jasmine start to laughing and hissing
her teeth about how his Mama and Papa would go crazy

to know that the boy following his father's path
and sniffing after some "nigger pussy," . . .

And you turned red and told her to be quiet,
and send me out to where children belong,

and wasn't two minutes before Aunt Jasmine was going,
head in the sky, backside rolling defiant,

with you shouting at her back, "I don't want
them children to feel that all white folks is bad!

They got better coming for them, that's all!"
And that was all I heard from you 'bout it.

Can't imagine what I'd a done when he come at me again,
if Aunt Jasmine didn't take me aside to tell me

not to let that cracker boy touch me
and not to mind you, Mama, 'cause she say

sometimes you wasn't too sure
which one of your kin you might meet on the way.

I gather all these memories inside me still,
and there's nothing to do but line them up

look them over, standing there like stations
of my crosses, and your crosses, Mama;

then I weep for love of you
weep for love of you, Mama.

Story Time

For you, love was the story
you told in the soft evenings,

your body remembering old contours
of embrace, the warmth of a man

in the midnight hour,
the smell of his armpit,

soil in his fingers,
carbolic on his skin.

You told of the seamstress,
tall, long-headed daughter of slaves

whose fingers would feed in whispers
cotton and silks into the slow chewing Singer,

her heel-and-toe action on the pedal,
as expert as the planting of rice seeds

in the thick mud of the St. Helena
where paddies spread green against blue;

making garments for only
the monied gentry. That woman

who would sing her solos in the fenced-in
altar of the A.M.E. church like she was alone

in this world, making the songs new,
stitching along a pattern dreamt up at nights,

making those old songs something else,
those old blood-stained songs.

You told of the white blacksmith,
burly man with whispy corn hair

and eyes so far into themselves
that you could only see sorrow

when he turned them on you
like some speechless beast—cow,

horse, sheep, goat, or passive pig
waiting stupidly to be slaughtered;

and you would tell how you always knew
that some white folks knew the blues, too.

You would tell this with tears,
this story of the man leaving

the gaol of his conjugal bed;
for sometimes, you said

those white folks married for nothing
but money and blood;

and his wife, a sickly thing,
weary of the world, hated him

for being a fool who never traveled,
never wanted to travel, never read a book,

just wanted to stay in the face of a furnace
till his face got all black like a slave;

she would call him a beast to his face,
an uncouth thing good for only one thing,

to root his way into her tender body
which was not made for carrying babies.

And he would walk soft through Sumter
nights, crossing the shining tracks

into the darkened belly of the other city
to find the seamstress, fingering her needles,

making magic with those bolts of cloth
that caught the lamplight and shimmered.

You could name all the fabrics,
love fabrics you called them,

crinoline, silk, chiffon, cotton,
burlap, khaki, corduroy, linen . . . .

In that closet of hues, they would whisper
love; he would offer the sorrow of his days,

calling back the tender memory
of a Nanny, long swollen by sugar and dead,

calling back the comforts of nurture milk
in this seamstress's voice, loving her

like that gentle way that only white folks know,
you said.
    And how one day they up

and left for Florence, how he lived
with her before the gaze of the town,

and they made the prettiest babies
you had ever laid eyes on: tall, nice hair

light water in their eyes. And I would watch
your eyes tear with love for this man, this

memory, telegraphing the tragedy,
evidence of a world not right.

The jealous, evil-eyed, bad-minded black folk
went whispering to his family in Sumter,

and that wife come to find her voice,
too scared now that he might marry

the seamstress; and just like that,
the world came down on him heavy;

his people talking about how he'd be cut off
from all that was his by blood.

You tell of the day he rode back to Sumter,
his seamstress standing stonefaced, silent.

Time could heal lots of things, you say,
but time couldn't make right what's gone so wrong.

The poor man turned to nothing in his soul,
turned in on himself and it killed him.

But he was a good man, a sweet man
always minding that seamstress and the boys.

Mama, you told the story, telling me
that fair-skin doctor was one of the sons,

a credit to his race, evidence of love,
for a child conceived in true love

could only turn out good, real good.
And with my Daddy gone, you taught me much

those day, Mama; and with your Daddy
not leaving a cent, much-less love,

denying everything springing that way
from his roving cock, I learnt something

those days, Mama. Your parable of integration,
best of both worlds, you call it;

but you are just a domestic,
and me a domestic's girl,

and I never dream of love like that,
because it made you sad to tell it, Mama,

and I hate to see you cry like that
for something you can't change no how.

Good Help

The house of the dead woman
flew half mast for two weeks;
shades all down and black,
the flowers drooping obediently,
and Jasmine the faithful domestic
would walk the slow drill of mourning,
burdened, her eyes carrying grief and loss
along the oak-lined avenue.
She'd stop to reminisce with poorly
Mrs. Mimms the cantankerous widow
who would rock on the porch
counting her last days among the leaves:
"I sure will miss her, m'am,
yes indeed, but she gone to a better place."
And all along the historical district
white folks would whisper about Jasmine,
about how you can't get help like that
these days, what with all those Northerners
coming to turn the heads of the black folk
who been living peaceably like this for centuries;
how you can't find help like this woman,
hoisting that flag half mast each day
to remember the woman who buttered her bread.

They never saw the red truck
cruising in the dead of night
to a squeaking standstill before the house
two nights running; never saw
Jasmine silently directing her sons
grunting with the weight of centuries
of collecting, collecting, collecting.
Never saw that truck wend its way
along the backroads of Carolina
towards a small Georgia shack
in the middle of pristine bush.
One day, the flag was not there no more
and Jasmine was sipping lemonade
on her cool porch, retired in Georgia.
There among that old furniture
all marinated and preserved by her
life blood and sweat; collectibles
she calls them, what she picked up
along the way. She is always laughing,
always nodding to her own head song:
"Praise the Lord for good help."

Grits

When my body aches with longing
for a man's shape and my sometimes man's

too stupid to know when a woman's tossing
all her up-bringing and circumspect ways

out into the damp night, giving up
her good sense, pragmatic Christian decorum

all for some good loving and the feel
of water swirling in her belly-bottom;

when I wake to a pale dawn,
the sky still stained with an old storm,

whimpering like sobs after the mauling
of the speckled limbed dogwood outside my window;

and I feel to crawl into your bed, Mama,
thick with the smell of Bengay,

mint ointment, old French talc and the stale
of your under-things laced with woman's scents;

I cook.
       I cook bacon back and with the grease,
scramble some eggs with milk, peppers, onions,

bake biscuits with sugar, fry chicken gizzards,
sweeten the black insides of my coffee

till it's thick as molasses and sharp,
and I turn me some grits—white soft love

in the pot, cooked long till this smell
of some childhood morning is you, always there

to hold me, to feed me, Mama, that soft belly
of grits, caressing everything awful and hard

to a watery, bland, dreamless porridge, like
unconditional love. And after, I smoke

and drift into the dream lake of bubbling
grits, softly cooing in my ears.

Was a time I would call you and cry on the phone.
These days, I work some grits and smoke.

Mother and Daughter

And when you came home at night,
you would step out the backdoor of the Ford
like the queen of England, with your pink
coat and your navy blue uniform; toss

back that gratitude-laced smile to them
who don't even look twice before high-tailing it out
of the area, like some ghosts are at their back;
and you'd watch the fading red lights, willing them safe passage.

Then your face would grow hard with fatigue
like a mask, and you would chew slow
the tepid meal I laid before you
and hold your jaw and stare

into the void of an insignificant radio drone.
I saw you and wondered what made you
gather your body each morning to go back,
and what made you gather the courage to come home.

Foolish, ungrateful child that I was,
I thought that maybe you had a choice,
that maybe you loved it there, loved them so
that if you could you would stay with them.

Some nights I wanted to give you a break
from the insipid yellow light of this hovel
and just send you back into the Ford, back
to that smile of something that looked like longing.

Sometimes, I was scared, while cooking,
that you wouldn't come home, would just
stay there, become one with them, love them,
free from the squalid monotony of our home.

I want to tell you this; that somehow
me with a son like a stone tied to me,
doing what I have to do to make ends meet,
I understand now that desire to run away, run away.

But pride stops me, or just a feeling that maybe
you would look at me with too much hurt;
you would call me the ungrateful heifer
you always knew me to be, and brush me off.

Circle

The torches dance in a circle
round the only electric light
in this wayside avenue.
Hear the horses snorting,
feel the thump in my heart
and my Mama holding me
and saying, "Never mind, girl,
they just making circles
around that lamp post,
and that's their right,
'cause it's their lamp post,
it's their electricity, not ours."

And when my chest would feel
like it would burst
from the sobbing,
she'd just smile
and say, "Your great-grand uncle
was a white soldier,
a captain, too
and they named this road
for him and his kin;
they know it,
they can see it
in your skin, don't fret."

And I would calm me down
dreaming of my ancestor,
riding hard with saber drawn
after the men in their sheets
and their flaming torches
circling the lamp-post.

Poems in Everyday Places

Your story told,
your poem made,

I, scavenger poet,
swoop and pick

at the living thing,
to make my own

feast of metaphor,
gourmet of irony.

He said those words,
spat them out in my face:

"Not as long as I live
will I see no colored child

riding a school bus."
Roosevelt looking down

like God almighty,
and the flag curled in the corner.

Well, he never saw them,
those colored children

climbing onto the yellow bus
books in hand, and riding,

but someone whispered it in his ear
while he stared into the black.

My mother said never rejoice
in the infirmities of others;

sometimes I let my mother down
and commit sins of the soul.

I am singing this song for him
and dancing on his grave:

"What you wish for,
that's what you're gonna get."

Four

Vengeance

School House

Nothing fancy, never fancy,
every board counted, every nail,

every bench, every piece of shingle,
nothing fancy, just love.

The hands of men with nothing but hope
in their fingers, tenderly grew this school

from the swamp-soft earth,
there under the canopy of ancient trees;

grew this sanctuary for learning,
a school where once there was bush.

And the children came,
soaked to the bone with morning rain

and the discriminating splatter of mud
by the wheels of the yellow school buses

ferrying the white children to their brick
edifice where they learned difference.

And we would wait with towels to ready them—
shaken but not broke—to learn.

There is nothing here, and here is a germ
of possibility. The wind wailed

late in nineteen forty-two,
and we trembled at the fate of the temple

while we held up the walls of our homes
straining against the blast outside.

In the early morning, when all was calm
we walked with tools, timber and fearful hearts

into the dense madness of the swamp
to find the school standing tall,

miraculously saved from the howl
and the crash of old rotting trees.

Come Monday morning, the children came,
faces aglow with new hope, new hope.

Vengeance

We wear our plans of vengeance
deep beneath the layers of normal life;

gentle handshakes, sweetly cologned,
always smiling "welcome in"; and sometimes

when we are not thinking about it
it is forgotten, as if the storehouse

of hurt was never there. Then in a wave
of memory, the wound smarts again

and we find the pulse of our hate
slowly gathering heat in the skin.

I placed a curse on a white man, once;
a silent curse I told to no one,

and you will never know the sweet
satisfaction of seeing him go blind,

decrepit and despondent in his waning years;
and I spoke my pleasure to no one.

For days, I woke with something oddly
pleasant, a lightness of hope renewed,

making the day an anticipated joy; during
all those lovable days I would laugh a lot.

The taste of vengeance is too sweet
for a heart of Christ. I repent. I sin.

Snapshot of the Southside

Integration's
a suction

draining us
of blood.

The remnant?
not pale

like a blooded
corpse,

but stark
and bare;

the gutted
carcass

of an old man
laid out to rest

in the drying
elements.

Sleep

In that twilight before sleep,
the in-between wash of mute light,

the television already a dream
fragment of colour against a pastiche

of winter field browns like old photographs
(memories come easy in this place),

the body slowly crumbles,
everything seeps from the bones,

all day, tensely waiting for the sweat
of sugarlessness, the heart's racing,

before the calming of hastily gobbled
mints, bonbons, chocolates, anything.

I try to suck, but the sugar is too slow
so I chew, crushing the stones of energy

into the fevered hunger of my blood,
waiting for the fix, waiting for the fix.

The sweet balm calms the riot,
calms the blood. In that lapse

there is a metaphor of a twilight
place of falling back,

no net to catch, just sinking.
I live for these small orgiastic pleasures.

At midnight, I wake startled by
the kick of my nervy legs.

The lamplight seems too yellow.
I listen for the intruder. He does not come.

In this interim, I stare at the seconds
switching in spastic efficiency

on the clock radio; I long for better days,
younger days of nights devoured by sleep.

Waking is the nightmare, now.
I move slowly to the turn-table.

Mahalia's voice scratches to live
buoyed by a wash of organs;

they wail, she wails, they drone
she drones. I stare into the sound

my eyes stoned into a dumb silence.
In this equinoctial quiet, I rest.

Fire Makers

In the ragged edge of winter,
the children tested the chill

like naked feet in an unknown pool,
then gathering what warmth

they could muster, they searched
the woods with eyes, familiar

with the texture of branches,
and found the dry pieces quickly,

carrying them cradled in their arms.
From the creaking porch,

I watched them return like creatures
birthed among the twisted trunks,

haloed by their rising breaths,
the leaves crackling underfoot.

And always, the flame would fade
only when the last lesson was learnt;

before the twilight six-mile trek
to the predictable labors of home.

"How much further, m'am?"
"Not much further, child, just beyond the bend."

Sanding

With sand paper
we scraped the traces
of their fingers,
stains of their carelessness;

memories of their rejection,
we sandpapered like a ritual
of love, making it clean,
this learning in a one-roomed school.

Hard to clean away
a legacy of bland indifference.
Once I scraped too deep;
beneath the colour, I found white,

the absence of meaning, a void
of imagination, the white of leprosy
like the bone-white skeleton of anomie.
I hid the scar from the children's eyes.

Gardening

She cultivates full-bodied roses,
pacing her body against July's heat,
humming her old melodies,

fingers sucking life from the giving soil,
old soil she has nurtured for decades,
eking blossoms while the world burned.

The street is not what it was,
but her eyes have seen worse.
Now the boys look up, bold-faced.

At day's end, she whispers to that man
long gone from this address,
just the colour of him in the sunset;

his shadow's familiar shape
looms, she smiles and mutters
at the Item's stories, a city in flux.

There are pages of stories
shaping themselves in her nimble mind.
She talks in pictures, we are enthralled.

In the old chapel, with timber
that cloistered slaves turned free,
her stories carry the cadence of miracles,

striking pragmatic magic in her wisdom;
we intone amens at her wan smile,
and sing triumphant old hymns.

Five

Obituaries

Obituaries

I scan the list of dead
daily, searching for names,
stories in my heart, I speak

them like a mantra, softly rolling
the language on my tongue,
eyeing in my head the faces

committing the travesty on me;
contemptuous gazes. I curse them,
and then role their names out.

As each passes, I count my days,
whisper my prayer of thanksgiving;
their grave is victory for me,

walking this earth after they
have shriveled and passed.
Though broken, though sweat-stained

with the heat of diabetic fevers,
though struggling to see through the haze
of my lidded eyes, a reptile's

film to protect me from seeing
the constant squalor of my people,
I count my days like I count my enemies

falling to the ravages of time.
And when my heart strains,
longing to burst and fly away home,

I rail against this darkness,
letting the names of the living foes,
cursed enemies who are hanging on

offer me silent strength,
the unspoken secret of longevity,
counting, counting, counting,

until, one day, the names
will be of younger ones, the duty
of some other warrior. Then I will sleep.

                                    Amen

Tall Man Flies

Gangly man, skin like red dirt,
you have let rip,
a streak of living
across these here United States.

Philadelphia, Detroit,
New York, like a curse,
Missouri, Washington.
When they saw you coming,

they cleared the jails.
Traveling man, it took nothing
for you to pick up
and follow the boy, King,

into batterings by sticks,
washings by spit,
beds of concrete,
crying "Freedom! Freedom!"

'Cause that nothing town
called curfew before the sun
was quite tired of it all
and they would lock you up.

Keep moving, nothing would slow
you down until, bone-weary
some flame of Pentecost
caught you and singed what little

hair was left
and gave you a voice
to preach in iambics
like in the old days.
You've got more years to go,
though the way words are found
has clouded some in your head,
the way thoughts make memory.

But all those years of letting rip
gave you psalms of penitence,
each day offered, a sin forgiven
a new song made, eyes clearing.

I can tell you've been talking
to the dead, the way you are startled
to find me before you, the way you expect
me to know the street you live on,

and every dream in your head
that you have not spoken to me,
but have said to those
you talk to at night.

I follow you to the Atlantic's edge,
then I let you go on ahead;
staring at your gangly flight,
old arms pointing homewards.

Wisteria is Kwame Dawes's eleventh collection of verse since he published *Progeny of Air* in 1994, which won the Forward Poetry Prize. He has published an additional eight antholgies and books of fiction, drama, and literary and cultural criticism. His awards include a Pushcart Prize, the Hollis Summers Poetry Prize and the Poetry Business Prize. His book *Bob Marley: Lyrical Genius* remains the most authorative study of the lyrics of Bob Marley. Dawes is the Distingusihed Poet-in-Residence at the University of South Carolina where he is Director of the South Carolina Poetry Initiative and the University of South Carolina Arts Institute. Dawes is Programming Director of the Calabash International Literary Festival.